500 Vintage Gold Ephemera Labels 1887
By C. Anders

As here shown, any Name, Dose or Poison, will be inserted, in any Label, at the prices quoted.   107

No. 4266—250, 35c; 500, 50c; 1000, 70c.

Fld. Ext. of
LOUIS HILMER,
Apothecary,
Cor. Geary and Larkin Sts., San Francisco.

No. 4267—250, 35c; 500, 50c; 1000, 70c.

W. R. YOUNG, Druggist,
ESSENCE PEPPERMINT
NATIONAL CITY, CAL.

No. 4268—250, 35c; 500, 50c; 1000, 70c.

LAUDANUM---Poison.

Three months old, - - 2 drops.	Ten years old, - - - 14 drops.
One year old, - - - 4 drops.	Twenty years old, - - 25 drops.
Four years old, - - - 6 drops.	Adults, - - - - - - 30 drops.

HENRY EARLE & CO., DRUGGISTS,
CANON CITY, COLORADO.

No. 4269—250, 35c; 500, 50c; 1000, 70c.

POISON.
C. W. JAMES, City Drug Store,
Main St., Baker City, Or.

No. 4270—250, 35c; 500, 50c; 1000, 70c.

No. 4271—250, 35c; 500, 50c; 1000, 70c.

From W. P. McDERMOTT,
DRUGGIST AND CHEMIST,
BLACK DRAUGHT.
Cor. 24th and Valencia Streets,
SAN FRANCISCO.

No. 4272—250, 35c; 500, 50c; 1000, 70c.

Pure Olive Oil.
—FROM—
H. C. FIDLER & CO.
Druggists and Apothecaries,
SANTA ANA, CAL.

No. 4273—250, 40c; 500, 60c; 1000, 80c.

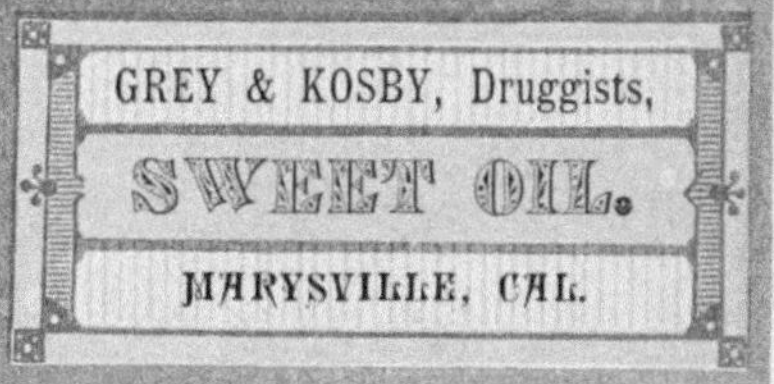

No. 4274—250, 40c; 500, 60c; 1000, 80c.

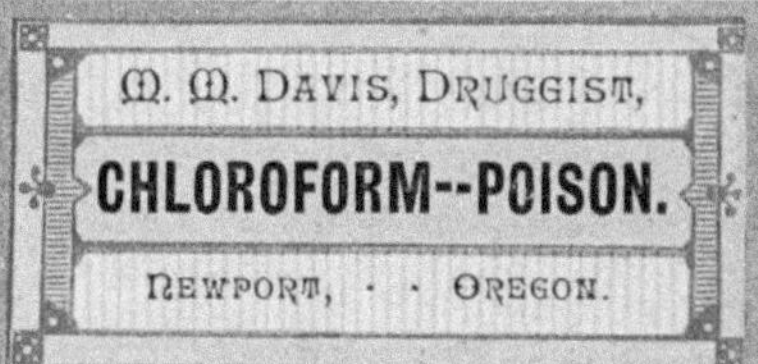

No. 4275—250, 35c; 500, 50c; 1000, 70c.

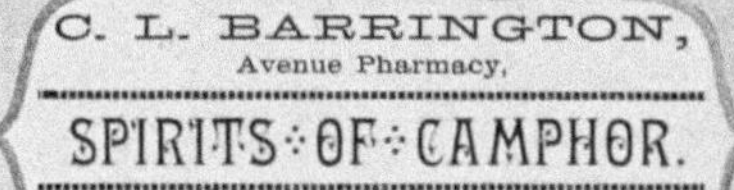

No. 4276—250, 35c; 500, 50c; 1000, 70c.

M. M. DAVIS, DRUGGIST,
CHLOROFORM--POISON.
NEWPORT, - - OREGON.

No. 4277—250, 35c; 500, 50c; 1000, 70c.

C. L. BARRINGTON,
Avenue Pharmacy,
SPIRITS OF CAMPHOR.
525 Montgomery Avenue,
SAN FRANCISCO.

No. 4278—250, 35c; 500, 50c; 1000, 70c.

N. T. CODY, Ventura Drug Store,
EPSOM SALTS.
San Buena Ventura, Cal.

No. 4279—250, 35c; 500, 50c; 1000, 70c.

No. 4280—250, 35c; 500, 50c; 1000, 70c.

TINCTURE OF IODINE.
C. McNABB & CO.,
Chemists and Apothecaries,
Cor. Riverside Avenue and Howard Street,
SPOKANE FALLS, W. T.

No. 4281—250, 35c; 500, 50c; 1000, 70c.

PAREGORIC.

ORDINARY DOSE.

Three days old, - 3 drops.	One year old, - - 13 drops.
One week old, - 5 drops.	Five years old, - 25 drops.
One month old, - 8 drops.	Adults, - 1 to 2 teaspoonfuls.

Repeat every two, three or four hours.

HENRY SENGSTACKEN, Druggist,
Eugene City, Oregon.

No. 4282—250, 35c; 500, 50c; 1000, 70c.

H. W. LITTLE, Practical Pharmacist,
HOLLAND GIN.
Main St., Lewiston, Idaho.

No. 4283—250, 35c; 500, 50c; 1000, 70c.

N. H. SHEPHERD,
Druggist and Apothecary,
PURE OLIVE OIL.
OPPOSITE DEPOT,
WHEATLAND, CAL.

No. 4284—250, 35c; 500, 50c; 1000, 70c.

CREOSOTE.
L. S. DARLAND,
The Post Office Drug Store,
MAIN ST.,
Yakima, Washington T'y.

No. 4285—250, 35c; 500, 50c; 1000, 70c.

TOOTH ACHE DROPS.
D. MORRIS & SON,
Dealers in Drugs and Stationery,
MAIN STREET,
SCIO, - OREGON.

No. 4286—250, 35c; 500, 50c; 1000, 70c.

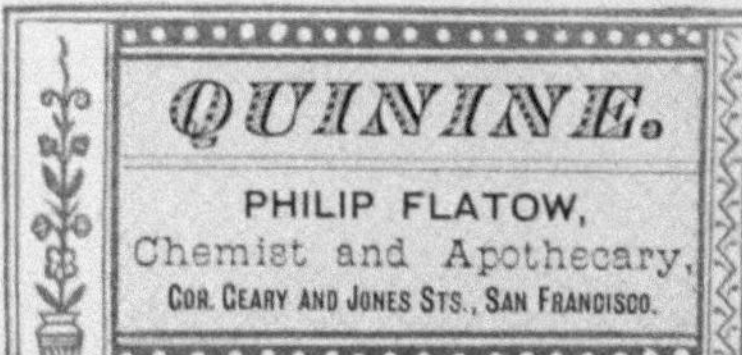

McNeil Bros., San Jose, Cal.

Dispensing Labels.

No. 4305—250, 60c; 500, 85c; 1000, $1.20.

O. H. P. CORNELIUS, Druggist,
TURNER, OREGON.

No.   Date,

M. D.

No. 4306—250, 70c; 500, 95c; 1000, $1.40.

CITY DRUG STORE. - WHITE & BAILEY, Proprietors,
Conn Street, Colton, Cal.

No.   Date,

Directions:

M. D.

No. 4307—250, 80c; 500, $1.10; 1000, $1.60.

WATKINS BROS., Druggists,
Kingman, Ariz. Ter.

No.   Date,

Directions:

M. D.

No. 4308—250, 60c; 500, 85c; 1000, $1.20.

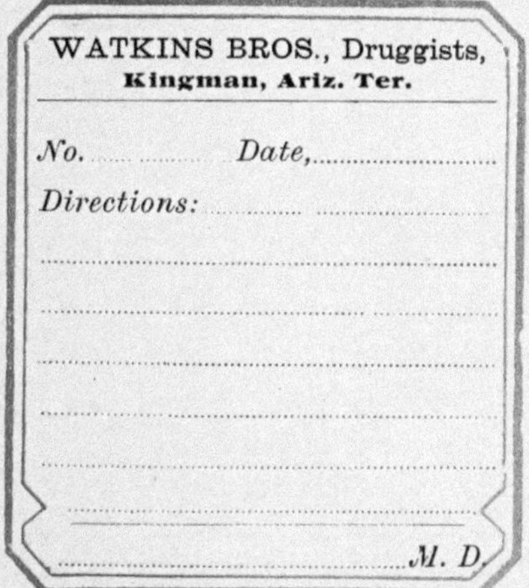

No. 4309—250, 70c; 500, 95c; 1000, $1.40.

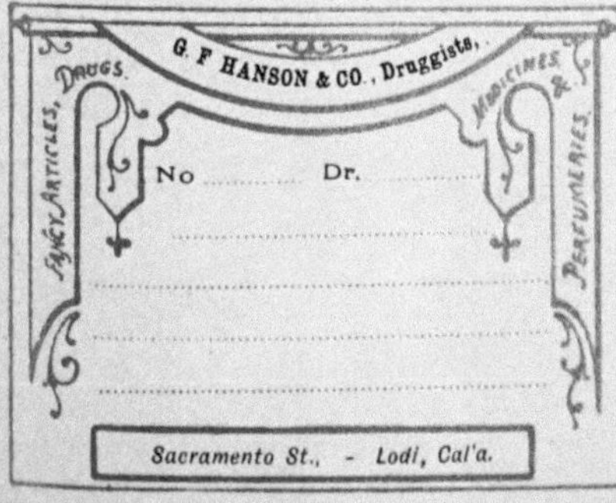

No. 4311—250, 60c; 500, 85c; 1000, $1.20.

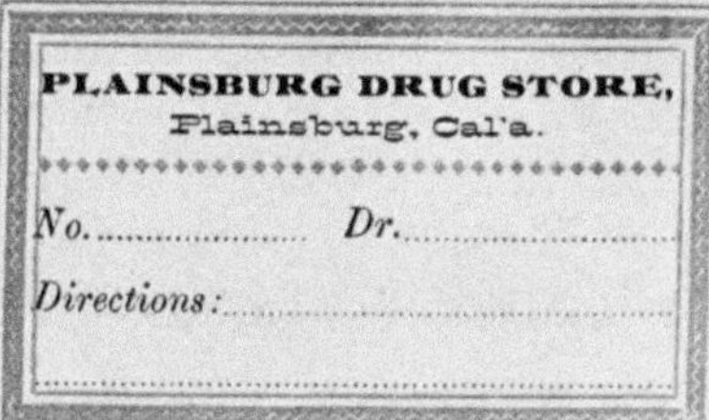

PLAINSBURG DRUG STORE,
Plainsburg, Cal'a.

No.   Dr.

Directions :

No. 4312—250, 70c; 500, 95c; 1000, $1.40.

BART MORGAN & CO., Druggists,
Market Street Block, Oakland, Cal.

No.   Dr.

Directions :

No. 4313—250, 80c; 500, $1.10; 1000, $1.60.

Directions: No.   Dr.

PLAINSBURG DRUG STORE,
PLAINSBURG, CAL.

No. 4310—250, 80c; 500, $1.10; 1000, $1.60.

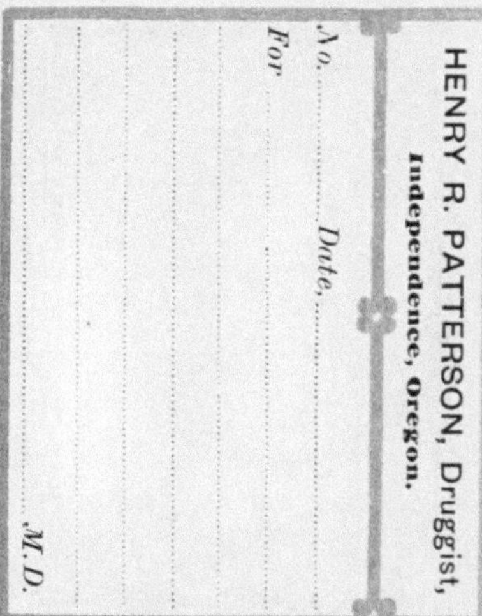

No. 4314—250, 60c; 500, 85c; 1000, $1.20.

RILEY & TRACY, Druggists and Apothecaries
Hailey, Wood River, Idaho.

No.   Date,
For

No. 4315—250, 70c; 500, 95c; 1000, $1.40.

Corner Drug Store, - JOE WARNER, Prop'r,
Elaine Block, Modesto, Cal.

No.   Date
For

M. D.

No. 4316—250, 80c; 500, $1.10; 1000, $1.60.

For   No.   Date,   M. D.

HENRY R. PATTERSON, Druggist,
Independence, Oregon.

In all Dispensing Labels, the words No., Dr., Date, For, Directions, Etc., can be printed, omitted or changed to suit. They can also be printed with or without dotted lines, as desired.

In case no changes are ordered in the wording or arrangement of Dispensing Labels, they will be left as here shown.

Owing to the heavy expense of getting up this Specimen Book, it is earnestly requested that it be not cut or mutilated in any way. In writing out your order it is only necessary to give the number of the Pattern, with any desired changes written out.

Dispensing Labels.

No. 4317—250, 60c; 500, 85c; 1000, $1.20.

No. 4318—250, 65c; 500, 90c; 1000, $1.30.

No. 4319—250, 75c; 500, $1.00; 1000, $1.50.

No. 4320—250, 85c; 500, $1.20; 1000, $1.70.

No. 4321—250, 40c; 500, 60c; 1000, 80c.

No. 4322—250, 70c; 500, 95c; 1000, $1.40.

No. 4323—250, 80c; 500, $1.10; 1000, $1.60.

No. 4324—250, 90c; 500, $1.25; 1000, $1.80.

No. 4325—250, 40c; 500, 60c; 1000, 80c.

No. 4326—250, 70c; 500, 95c; 1000, $1.40.

No. 4327—250, 80c; 500, $1.10; 1000, $1.60.

No. 4328—250, 90c; 500, $1.25; 1000, $1.80.

In all Dispensing Labels, the words No., Dr., Date, For, Directions, Etc., can be printed, omitted, or changed to suit. They can also be furnished with or without dotted lines, as desired. In case no changes are ordered in the wording or arrangement of Dispensing Labels, they will be left as here shown.

NOTE.

In this class of work we use four shades of coloring for Tint Grounds, viz: Green, Blue, Pink and Slate colors. Our aim is to assort them, but as this cannot always be done, we do not undertake to furnish any particular Tint exclusively, or to give the same shade of Tint a second time.

Dispensing Labels.

No. 4329—250, 40c; 500, 60c; 1000, 80c.

CH. G. BERGER, Druggist and Apothecary,
Corner Union and Larkin Streets, San Francisco.

No. 4330—250, 70c; 500, 95c; 1000, $1.40.

No.......... Date,

Dr.

F. J. SCHNEIDER, Druggist,
Main Street. - - Eureka, Nevada.

No. 4331—250, 85c; 500, $1.20; 1000, $1.70.

No.
Date.
F. J. SCHNEIDER, Druggist,
MAIN STREET, - EUREKA, NEV.
Dr.

No. 4332—250, 70c; 500, 95c; 1000, $1.40.

G. F. HANSON & CO., Druggists,
FANCY ARTICLES, DRUGS, MEDICINES & PERFUMERIES.
Sacramento St., - Lodi, Cal'a.

No. 4333—250, 80c; 500, $1.10; 1000, $1.60.

G F HANSON & CO., Druggists,
FANCY ARTICLES, DRUGS, MEDICINES & PERFUMERIES.
No   Dr.
Sacramento St., - Lodi, Cal'a.

No. 4335—250, 65c; 500, 90c; 1000, $1.30.

CITY DRUG STORE, E. J. JOLLY, M'gr,
PLACERVILLE, CAL'A.
No...................... Dr. ....
Directions: ....

No. 4336—250, 75c; 500, $1.00; 1000, $1.50.

CITY DRUG STORE, E. J. JOLLY, Manager,
PLACERVILLE, CAL'A.
No...................... Dr. ....
Directions: ....

No. 4337—250, 85c; 500, $1.20; 1000, $1.70.

CITY DRUG STORE, E. J. JOLLY, Manager.
PLACERVILLE, CAL'A.
No.
Directions:
Dr.

No. 4334—250, 90c; 500, $1.25; 1000, $1.80.

G. F. HANSON & CO., Druggists,
FANCY ARTICLES, DRUGS, MEDICINES & PERFUMERIES.
No.   Dr.
Sacramento St., - Lodi, Cal'a.

No. 4338—250, 65c; 500, 90c; 1000, $1.30.

C. H. DARROUGH, Apothecary,
Opp. Tremont Block, Red Bluff, Cal.
No.......... Dr. ....
Directions: ....

No. 4339—250, 75c; 500, $1.00; 1000, $1.50.

City Drug Store, - HENRY EARLE & CO.,
Canon City, Colorado.
No.
Dr.
Directions:

No. 4340—250, 90c; 500, $1.25; 1000, $1.80.

SECORD & BRUNTON, Druggists and Apothecaries,
No. 210 South First Street, San Jose, Cal.
No
Dr.
Directions:

In all Dispensing Labels, the words No., Dr., Date, For, Directions, Etc., can be printed, omitted, or changed to suit. They can also be furnished with or without dotted lines, as desired. In case no changes are ordered in the wording or arrangement of Dispensing Labels, they will be left as here shown.

NOTE—In this class of work we use four shades of coloring for Tint Grounds, viz: Green, Blue, Pink and Slate colors. Our aim is to assort them, but as this cannot always be done, we do not undertake to furnish any particular Tint exclusively or to give the same shade of Tint a second time.

Dispensing and Address Labels.

No. 4353—250, 70c; 500, 95c; 1000, $1.40.

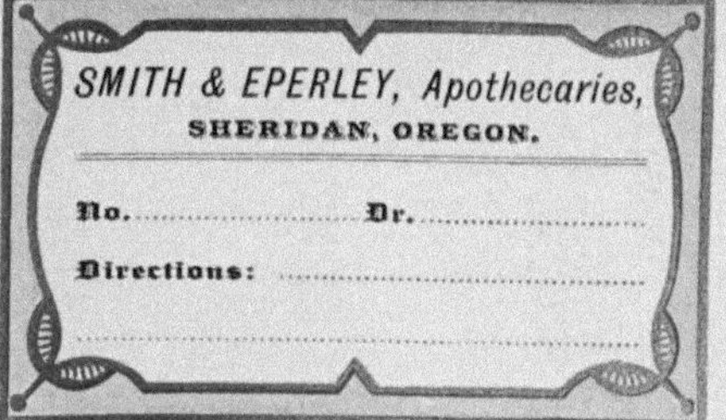

In all Dispensing Labels, the words No., Dr., Date, For, Directions, Etc., can be printed, omitted, or changed to suit. They can also be furnished with or without dotted lines, as desired. In case no changes are ordered in the wording or arrangement of Dispensing Labels, they will be left as here shown.

No. 4356—250, 70c; 500, 95c; 1000, $1.40.

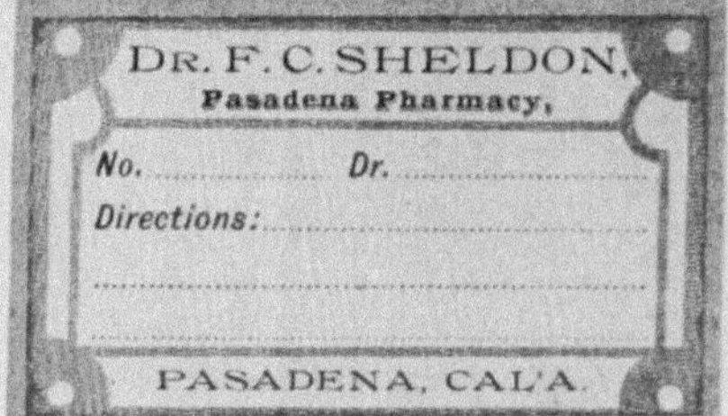

No. 4354—250, 80c; 500, $1.10; 1000, $1.60.

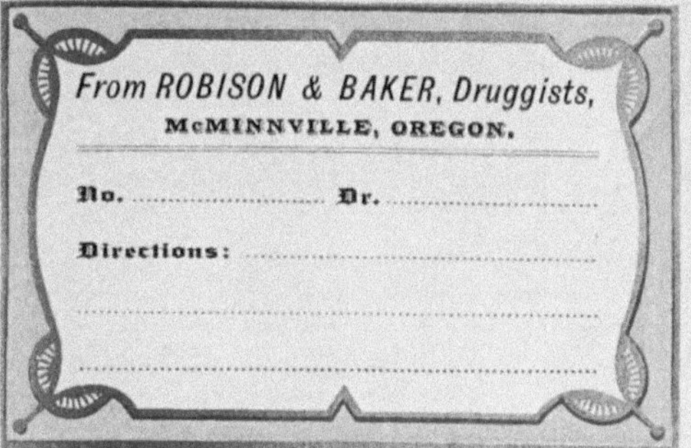

NOTE.

In this class of work we use four shades of coloring for Tint Grounds, viz: Blue, Green, Pink and Slate colors. Our aim is to assort them, but as this cannot always be done, we do not undertake to furnish any particular Tint exclusively, or to give the same shade of Tint a second time.

No. 4357—250, 80c; 500, $1.10; 1000, $1.60.

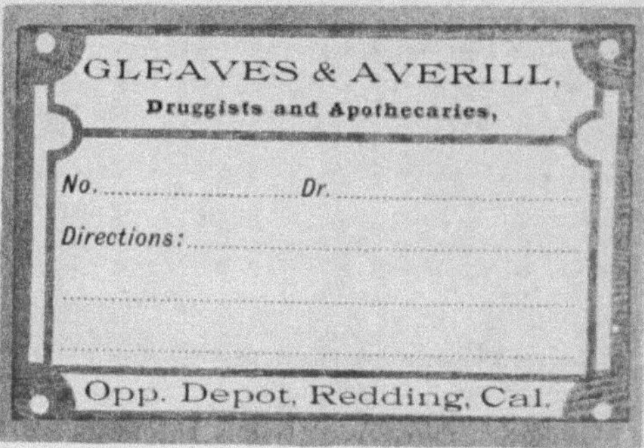

No. 4355—250, 90c; 500, $1.25; 1000, $1.80.

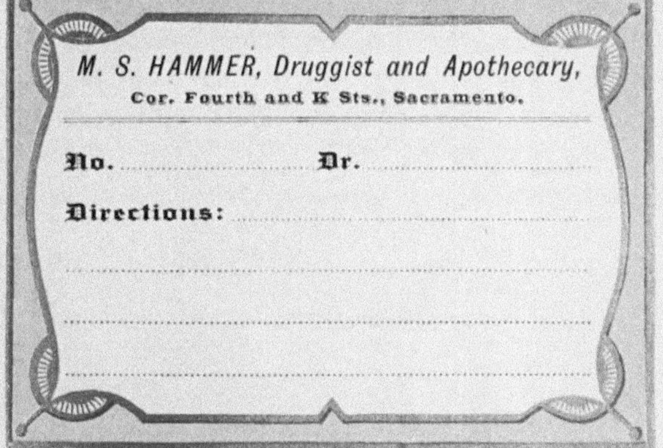

No. 4358—250, 90c; 500, $1.25; 1000, $1.80.

No. 4359.
250, 45c; 500, 65c; 1000, 90c.

No. 4362.
250, 30c; 500, 45c; 1000, 60c.

No. 4365.
250, 35c; 500, 50c; 1000, 70c.

No. 4369—250, 50c; 500, 70c; 1000, $1.00.

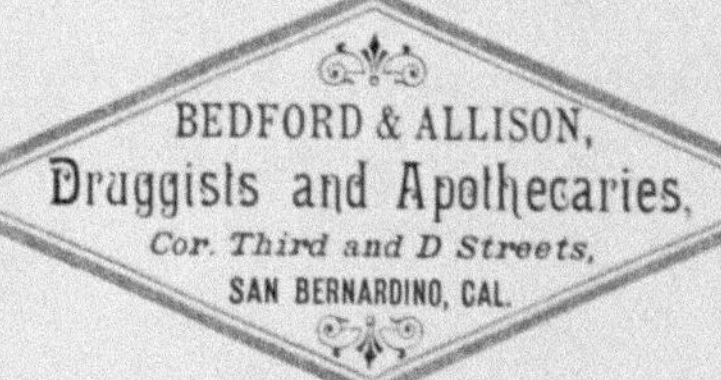

No. 4360.
250, 40c; 500, 60c; 1000, 80c

No. 4363.
250, 25c; 500, 35c; 1000, 50c.

No. 4364.
250, 30c; 500, 45c; 1000, 60c.

No. 4366.
250, 40c; 500, 60c; 1000, 80c.

These Labels are trimmed close to borders, and put up with rubber bands in packages of 250 each, ready for use.

DO NOT cut or mutilate this book, but order by NUMBER OF THE LABEL.

No. 4370—250, 45c; 500, 65c; 1000, 90c.

No. 4361.
250, 35c; 500, 50c; 1000, 70c.

No. 4367
250, 45c; 500, 65c; 1000, 90c.

No. 4368—250, 50c; 500, 70c; 1000, $1.00.

No. 4371—250, 40c; 500, 60c; 1000, 80c

Pill and Toilet Labels.

No. 4287—250, 50c; 500, 70c; 1000, $1.00.

No. 4288—250, 55c; 500, 75c; 1000, $1.10.

No. 4289—250, 60c; 500, 85c; 1000, $1.20.

No. 4290—250, 65c; 500, 90c; 1000, $1.30.

No. 4291—250, 75c; 500, $1.00; 1000, $1.50.

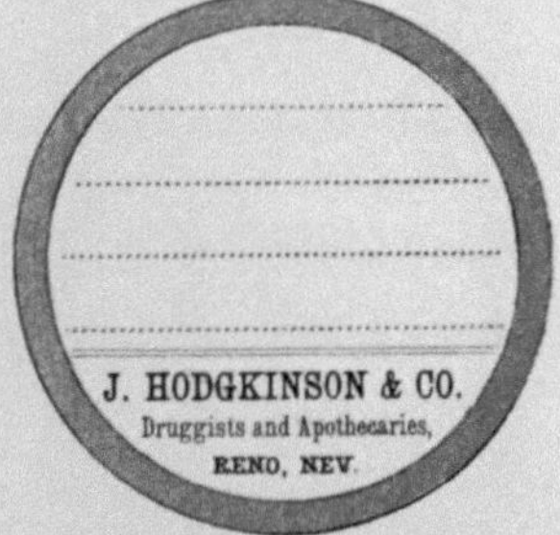

No. 4292—250, 85c; 500, $1.20; 1000, $1.70.

No. 4293—250, 55c; 500, 75c; 1000, $1.10.

No. 4294—250, 60c; 500, 85c; 1000, $1.20.

No. 4295—250, 65c; 500, 90c; 1000, $1.30.

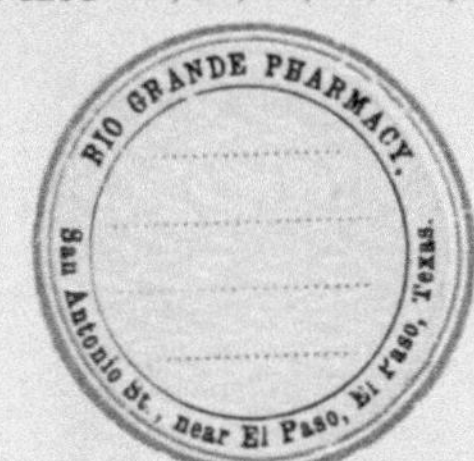

No. 4296—250, 70c; 500, 95c; 1000, $1.40.

No. 4297—250, 80c; 500, $1.10; 1000, $1.60.

No. 4298—250, 90c; 500, $1.25; 1000, $1.80.

No. 4299.
250, 55c; 500, 75c; 1000, $1.10.

No. 4300.
250, 65c; 500, 90c; 1000, $1.30.

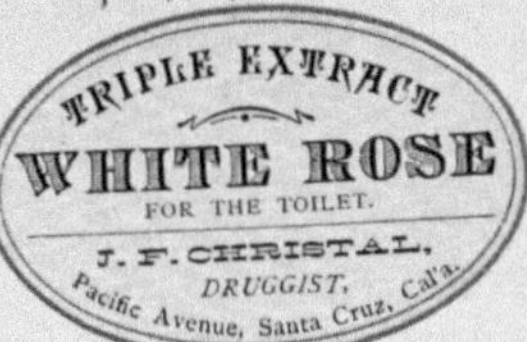

No. 4301—250, 75c; 500, $1.00; 1000, $1.50.

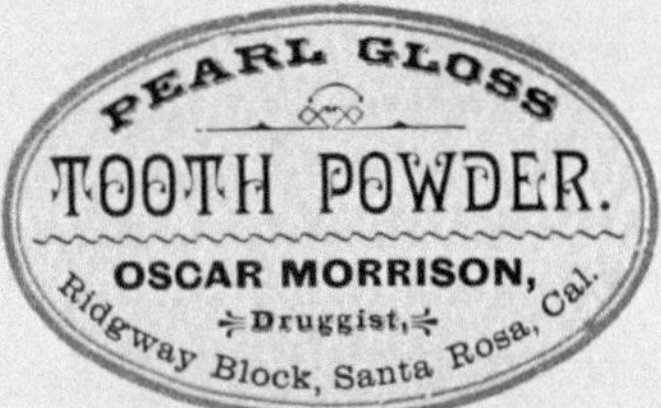

No. 4302—250, 90c; 500, $1.25; 1000, $1.80.

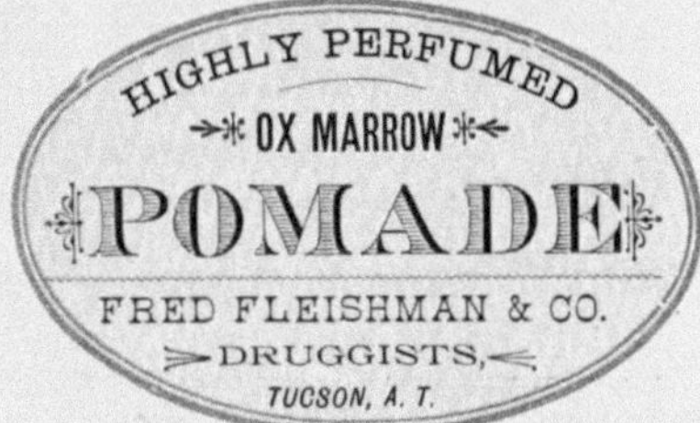

No. 4303—250, $1.00; 500, $1.40; 1000, $2.00.

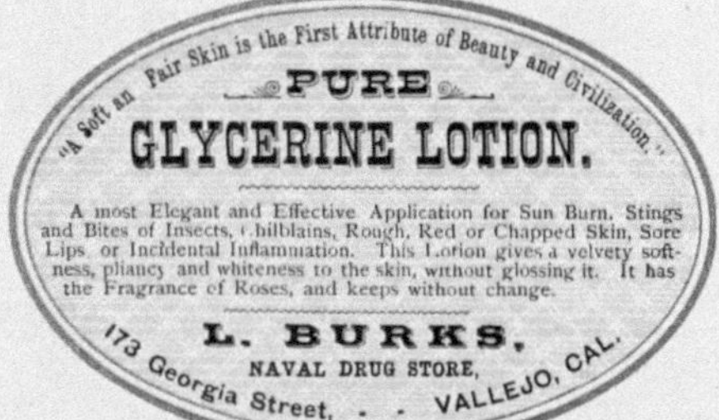

No. 4304—250, $1.25; 500, $1.75; 1000, $2.50.

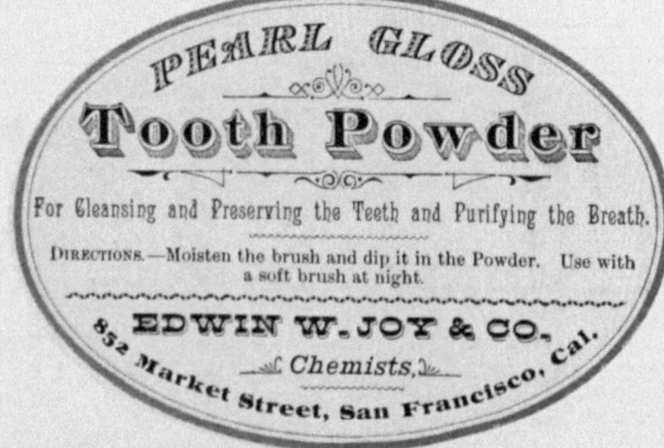

All Pill Labels can be printed with or without lines for
writing on, No., Dr., Date, For, Directions, Etc., at the prices
quoted. Unless changes are ordered, they will be left as
here shown.

All Round and Oval Labels are cut close to borders, by
machinery, without extra charge.

In any of the Labels shown on this page the name of
the article will be changed without extra charge, but
where an entire change of wording is ordered, a slight
advance (sufficient to cover the additional labor) will be
added to the prices here given.

DO NOT cut or mutilate this Specimen Book, but order
by Number of Pattern, and write out changes desired.

No. 4378—250, $1.25; 500, $1.75; 1000, $2.50.

CONCENTRATED
ESSENCE
—OF—
JAMAICA GINGER

This Essence is warranted to possess, in a concentrated form, all the valuable properties of JAMAICA GINGER, and will be found, on trial, an excellent Family Medicine, being a most efficient remedy for Sick Headache, Indigestion, Colic, Nervous Debility, Cholera Morbus and Cholera.

DIRECTIONS.— A teaspoonful immediately after meals will most generally relieve Indigestion. In acute cases of pain or incipient Cholera, a teaspoonful may be given every half hour in sugar and water.

PREPARED BY
R. S. MARKELL, M. D.
Druggist and Bookseller,
CLOVERDALE, CAL.

No. 4379—250, $1.25; 500, $1.75; 1000, $2.50.

ROSE ✢ COLD ✢ CREAM
WITH
GLYCERINE

This Elegant Preparation, containing Pure Glycerine, is more soothing and healing, and much more pleasant to use (being less greasy), than the article commonly sold.

PREPARED ONLY BY
BENSON, SMITH & CO.
Pharmacists,
HONOLULU, H. I.

No. 4382—250, 80c; 500, $1.10; 1000, $1.60.

SAPONACEOUS
DENTINE
PREPARED AT
CRYSTAL DRUG STORE.
Corner 21st and Valencia Streets,
SAN FRANCISCO.

No. 4380—250, $1.25; 500, $1.75; 1000, $2.50.

✢ NOTE. ✢

A feature of this Series of Labels is its adaptability to all kinds of fine work. Indeed, any Label shown in Black Ink can be printed in this style by printing the border in Gold and the reading matter in Black Ink.

No. 4381—250, 75c; 500, $1.00; 1000, $1.50.

PEARL GLOSS
TOOTH POWDER
For Cleansing and Preserving the Teeth.
STEYLAARS & ROSSI, Chemists and Druggists,
N. E. Cor. Dupont St. and Montgomery Ave., S. F.

| No. 4383. | No. 4384. | No. 4385—250, $1.00; | No. 4386. | No. 4387. |
| 250, $1.35; 500, $1.90; 1000, $2.75. | 250, $1.25; 500, $1.75; 1000, $2.50. | 500, $1.40; 1000, $2.00. | 250, $1.50; 500, $2.00; 1000, $3.00. | 250, $1.25 500, $1.75; 1000, $2.50. |

SUPERIOR
FRENCH
COLOGNE
For the Toilet
H. B. SHAW,
Druggist,
SUTTER AND POWELL STS. S. F.

CONCENTRATED
EXTRACT
—OF—
LEMON
FOR FLAVORING
Ice Cream, Custards,
Pastry, Jellies, Etc.
PREPARED BY
J. L. ARMSTRONG
Druggist,
FRESNO, CAL.

Read carefully the preceding page before ordering from this Series. We do not print a less number than 250 to any one name.

Miscellaneous Labels.

No. 4405—250, $1.10; 500, $1.60; 1000, $2.25.   No. 4406—250, 85c; 500, $1.20; 1000, $1.70.   No. 4407—250, $1.10; 500, $1.60; 1000, $2.25.   No. 4408—250, 90c; 500, $1.25; 1000, $1.80.

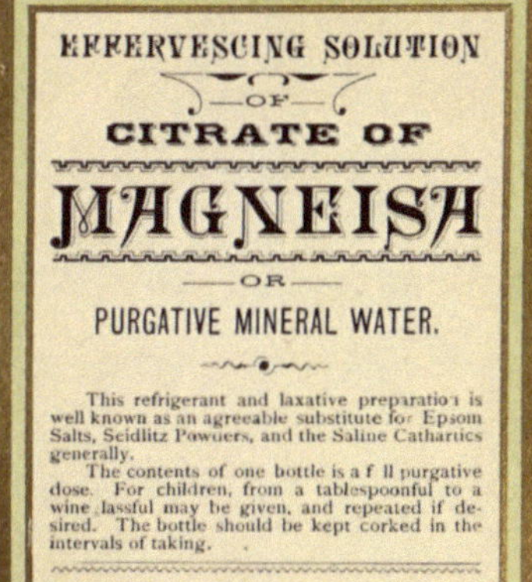

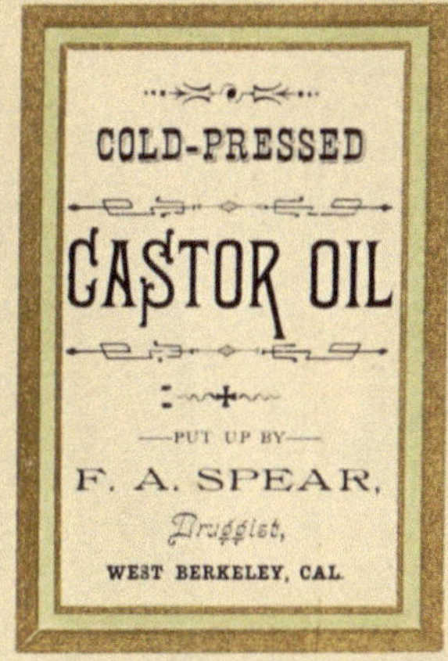

DO NOT
Cut or Mutilate this Book,
But Order by Number of Pattern.

No. 4409—250, 80c; 500, $1.10; 1000, $1.60.   No. 4410—250, 80c; 500, $1.10; 1000, $1.60.   No. 4411—250, 80c; 500, $1.10; 1000, $1.60.   No. 4412—250, 80c; 500, $1.10; 1000, $1.60.

No. 4413.
250, $1.75; 500, $2.35; 1000, $3.50.

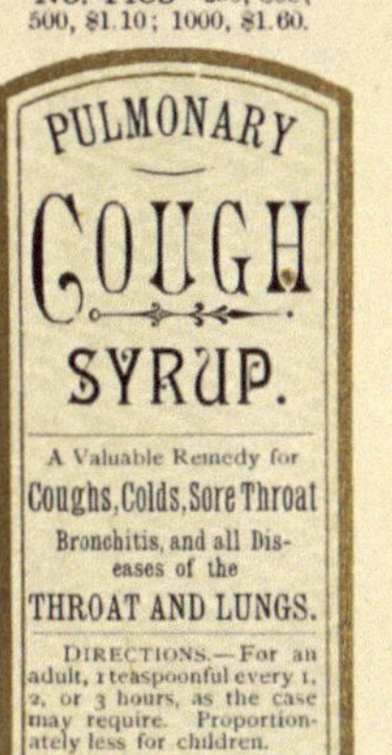

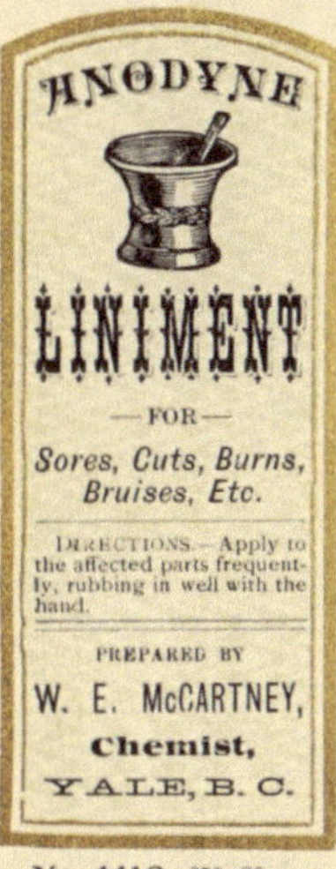

No. 4414.
250, $1.25; 500, $1.75; 1000, $2.50.   No. 4415.
250, $1.00; 500, $1.40; 1000, $2.00.   No. 4416—250, 80c; 500, $1.10; 1000, $1.60.

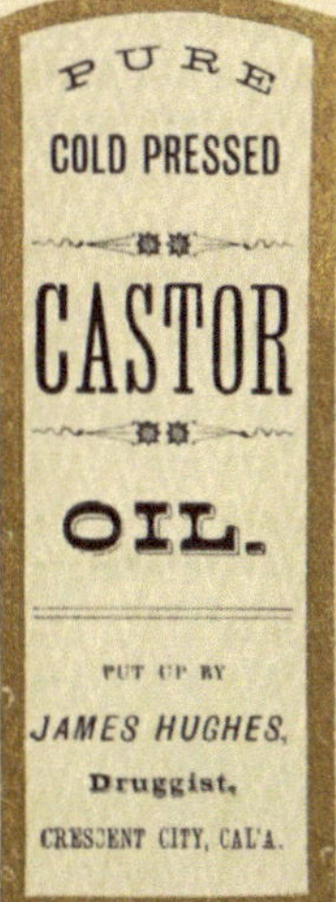

NOTE.—In this class of work we use four shades of coloring for Tint Grounds, viz: Green, Blue, Pink and Slate colors. Our aim is to assort them, but as this cannot always be done, we do not undertake to furnish any particular tint exclusively, or to give the same shade of tint a second time.

In any of the Labels shown on this page, the Name of Article will be changed without extra charge; but where an entire change of wording is ordered, a slight advance, (sufficient to cover the additional labor), will be charged. Other sizes of any Labels can also be furnished when desired

Miscellaneous Labels.

No. 4448. Kept in Stock at 8c per 100.

FOR EXTERNAL USE ONLY.

No. 4449. Kept in Stock a 8c per 100.

FOR OUTWARD APPLICATION.

No. 4450. Kept in Stock at 8c per 100.

GLASS. HANDLE WITH CARE.

No. 4451. Kept in Stock at 8c per 100.

HANDLE WITH CARE.

No. 4452. Kept in Stock at 8c per 100.

NOT TO BE TAKEN.

No. 4453. Kept in Stock at 8c per 100.

POISON. BE CAREFUL!

No. 4454. Kept in Stock at 8c per 100.

POISON. BEWARE!

No. 4455. Kept in Stock at 8c per 100.

SHAKE THE BOTTLE.

No. 4456. Kept in Stock at 8c per 100.

SHAKE BOTTLE BEFORE POURING OUT.

No. 4457. Kept in Stock at 8c per 100.

SHAKE THE VIAL.

No. 4458. Kept in Stock at 8c per 100.

SHAKE WELL BEFORE USING.

No. 4459. Kept in Stock at 8c per 100.

SOLD FOR MEDICINAL USE ONLY.

No. 4460. Kept in Stock at 8c per 100.

USE ONLY AS DIRECTED.

No. 4461. Kept in Stock at 8c per 100.

SHAKE THE BOTTLE BEFORE THE MEDICINE IS POURED OUT.

No. 4462. Kept in Stock at 8c per 100.

CAUTION. Be careful to keep this medicine out of the way of children, and not where food is kept.

No. 4463.
250, 75c; 500, $1.00; 1000, $1.50.

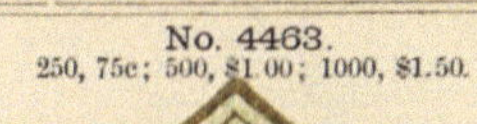
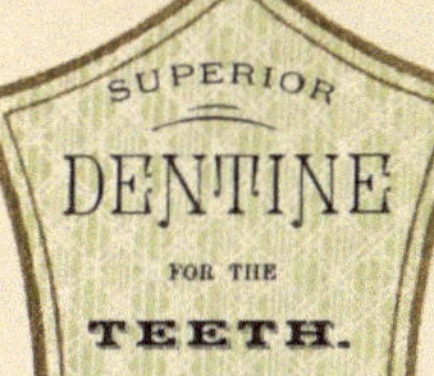

No. 4464.
250, 75c; 500, $1.00; 1000, $1.50.

No. 4465.
250, 75c; 500, $1.00; 1000, $1.50.

No. 4466—250, $1.00; 500, $1.40; 1000, $2.00.

No. 4467—250, 75c; 500, $1.00; 1000, $1.50.

No. 4468. 10c per 100.

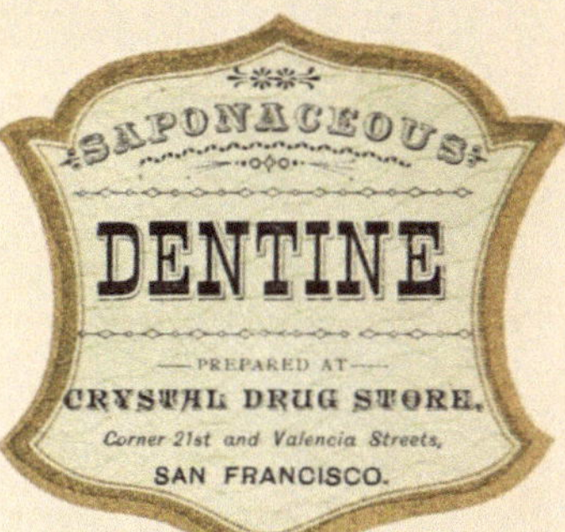

No. 4469. 10c per 100.

No. 4470. 10c per 100.

CAUTION.

As the sale of Poisonous substances is always attended with risk, it is earnestly requested that this preparation may be kept away from children, and not where food is kept.

No. 4471. 10c per 100.

KEROSENE OIL—Caution!

Do not attempt to light a fire with this Oil, and never fill the lamp while *burning*, or at *night*. Fill and trim the lamp daily, by daylight, occasionally emptying to clean. Keep the Oil in a *cool place*, away *from fire or unusual heat.* Neglect of these directions may cause loss of life, or prove otherwise disastrous.

No. 4472.
250, $1.00; 500, $1.40; 1000, $2.00.

No. 4473—250, 75c; 500, $1.00; 1000, $1.50.

NOTE.—In this class of work we use four shades of coloring for Tint Grounds, viz: Green, Blue, Pink and Slate colors. Our aim is to assort them, but as this cannot always be done, we do not undertake to furnish any particular tint exclusively, or to give the same shade of tint a second time.

McNeil Bros., San Jose, Cal.

116

Flavoring Extract Labels.

No. 4388.	No. 4389.	No. 4390.	No. 4391.	No. 4392.
250, $1.00; 500, $1.40; 1000, $2.00.	250, 90c; 500, $1.25; 1000, $1.80.	250, $1.00; 500, $1.40; 1000, $2.00.	250, 90c; 500, $1.25; 1000, $1.80.	250, $1.00; 500, $1.40; 1000, $2.00.

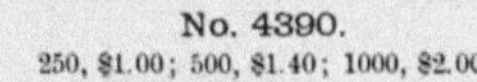

No. 4393.	No. 4394.	No. 4395.	No. 4396.	No. 4397.	No. 4398.

Nos. 4393 to 4398—250, 80c; 500, $1.10; 1000, $1.60.

No. 4399.	No. 4400.	No. 4401.	No. 4402.	No. 4403.	No. 4404.
				250, 75c; 500, $1.10; 1000, $1.50.	250, 75c; 500, $1.10; 1000, $1.50.

Nos. 4399 to 4402—250, 80c; 500, $1.10; 1000, $1.60.

In the Labels shown on this page the names of any Flavoring Extracts can be printed at the prices here quoted.

To save inquiries we would state that, at the prices here quoted, these Labels are only furnished as here shown. That is, on Nos. 4388 to 4392, the Fruits are NOT colored. If Fruits are wanted colored, order from pages 86 or 87.

Miscellaneous Labels.

No. 4417.
250, $1.00; 500, $1.40; 1000, $2.00.

No. 4418.
250, $1.25; 500, $1.75; 1000, $2.50.

No. 4419—250, $2.00; 500, $2.80; 1000, $4.00.

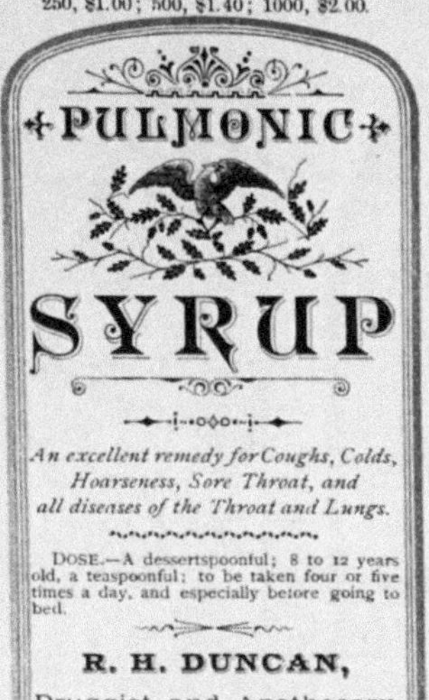

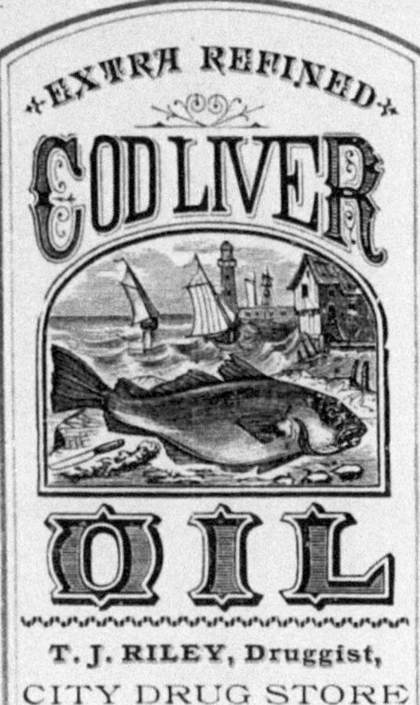

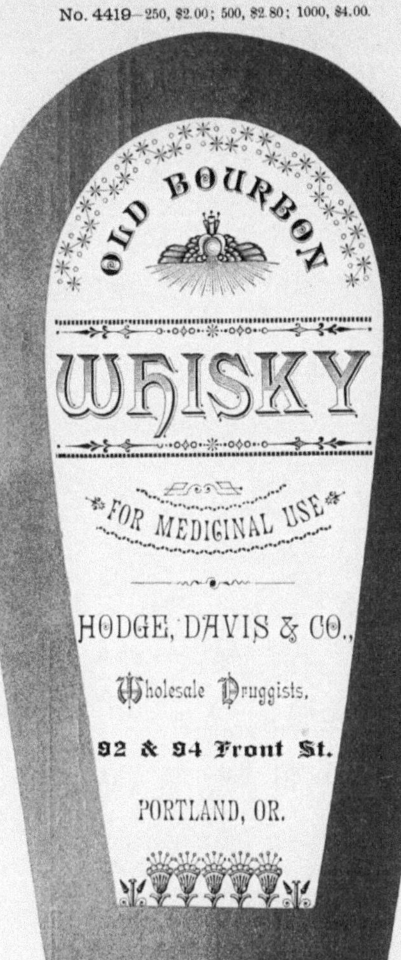

No. 4420.
250, 75c; 500, $1.00;
1000, $1.50.

No. 4421.
250, 80c; 500, $1.10; 1000, $1 60.

No. 4422.
250, 90c; 500, $1.25; 1000, $1.80.

No. 4425—250, 75c;
500, $1.00; 1000, $1.50.

No. 4426—250, 80c;
500, $1.10; 1000, $1.60.

In this class of work we use four shades of coloring for Tint
Grounds, viz: Pink, Blue, Green and Slate colors. Our aim is to
assort them, but as this cannot always be done, we do not undertake to furnish any particular tint exclusively, or to give the same
shade of tint a second time.

No. 4423—250, 80c; 500, $1.10; 1000, $1.60.

No. 4424—250, 90c; 500, $1.25; 1000, $1.80.

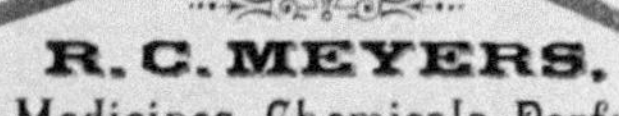

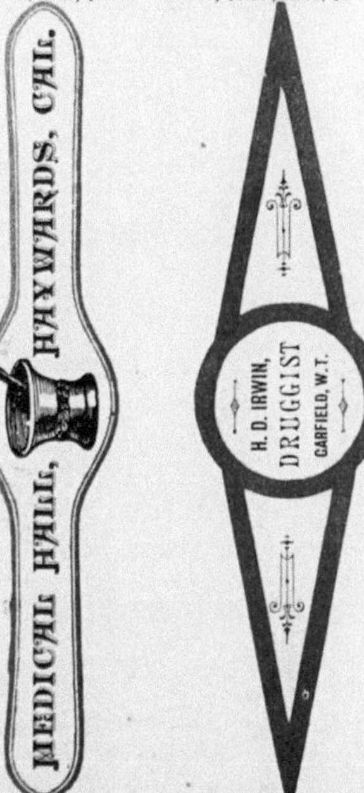

McNeil Bros., San Jose, Cal.

Toilet Labels.

No. 4427—250, $1.50; 500, $2.00; 1000, $3.00.

No. 4428—250, $1.25; 500, $1.75; 1000, $2.50.

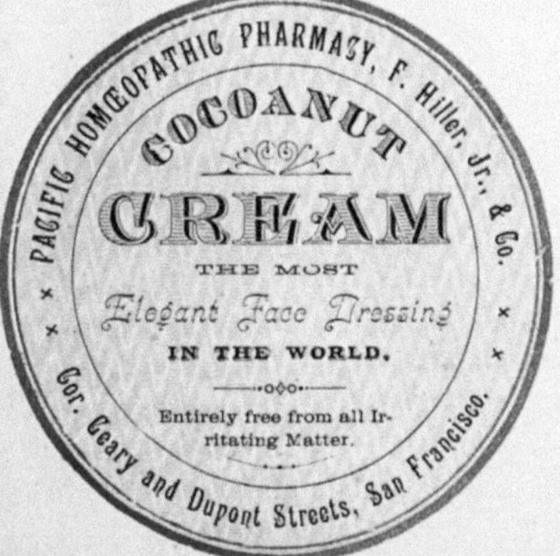

No. 4429—250, $1 10; 500, $1.60; 1000, $2.25.

No. 4430—250, 60c; 500, 85c; 1000, $1.20.

The Round Labels shown on this page, also Nos. 4431 to 4434, are trimmed close to borders by machinery without extra charge.

No. 4431—250, $1.00; 500, $1.40; 1000, $2.00.

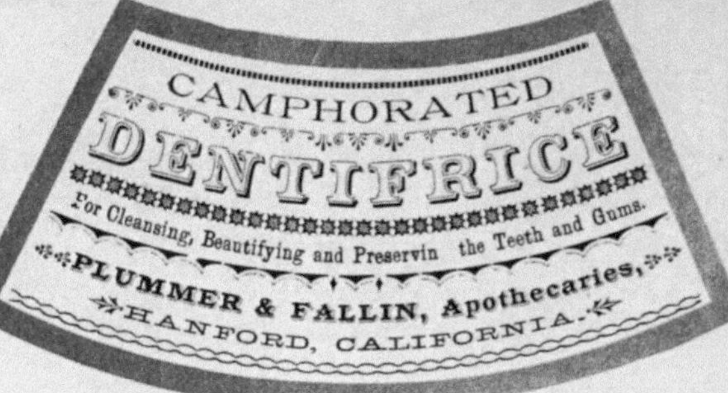

No. 4432—250, 75c; 500, $1.00; 1000, $1.50.

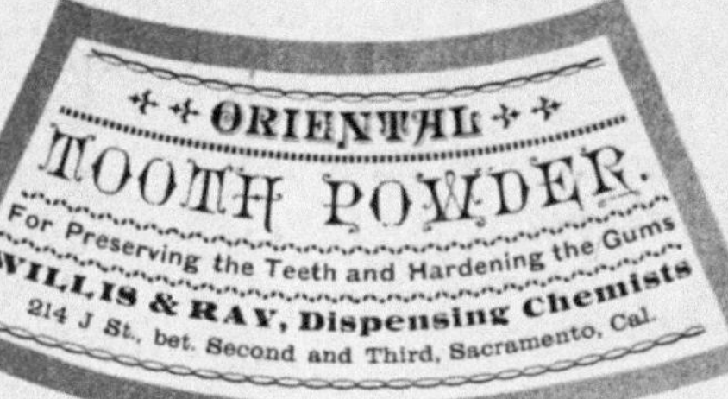

No. 4433 —250, $1.50; 500, $2.00; 1000, $3.00.

No. 4434.
250, 75c; 500, $1.00; 1000, $1.50.

No. 4435.
250, 50c; 500, 75c; 1000, $1.00.

No. 4436.
250, 75c; 500, $1.00; 1000, $1.50.

No. 4437—250, 75c; 500, $1.00; 1000, $1.50.

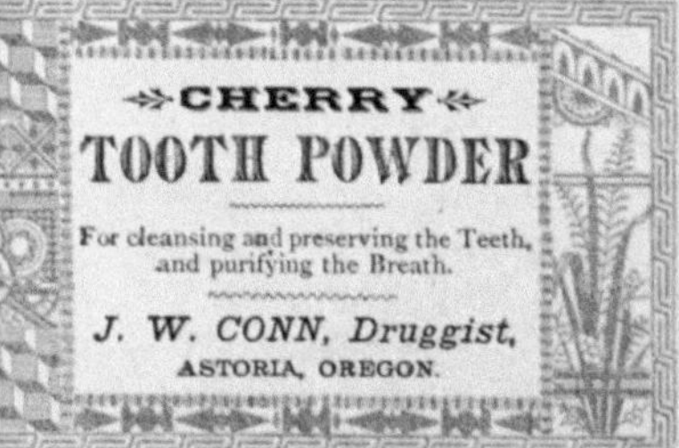

NOTE.—In this class of work we use four shades of coloring for Tint Grounds, viz: Pink, Blue, Green and Slate colors. Our aim is to assort them, but as this cannot always be done, we do not undertake to furnish any particular tint exclusively, or to give the same shade of tint a second time.

No. 4441—25c per 100.   No. 4442—25c per 100.   No. 4444—250, $1.25; 500, $1.75; 1000, $2.50.

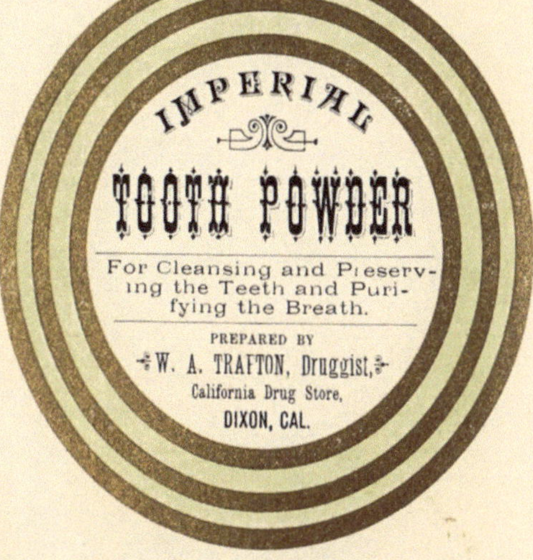

Superior Hair Oil, in above Pattern, at same Price.

No. 4443. 15c per 100.

No. 4445. 40c per 100.

*DO NOT Cut or Mutilate this Specimen Book, but order
by Number of the Pattern.*

No. 4447. 30c per 100.

No. 4446. 20c per 100.

NOTE.—In this class of work we use four shades of coloring for Tint Grounds, viz: Green,
Blue, Pink and Slate colors. Our aim is to assort them, but as this cannot always be done,
we do not undertake to furnish any particular tint exclusively, or to give the same shade
of tint a second time.

Liquor Labels.

No. 4498. Kept in Stock, as follows: 50, 40c; 100, 70c; 200, $1.15; 500, $2.25; 1000, $4.00.
We do not furnish these Labels in small quantities to a name at the wholesale rate. In other words, where but 50 or 100 labels *to a name* are wanted, each lot will cost 40c and 70c.

On above pattern, the names of all Whiskies and Brandies kept in Stock.

No. 4499—250, $1.25; 500, $1.75; 1000, $2.50. We do not print less than 250 to a name.

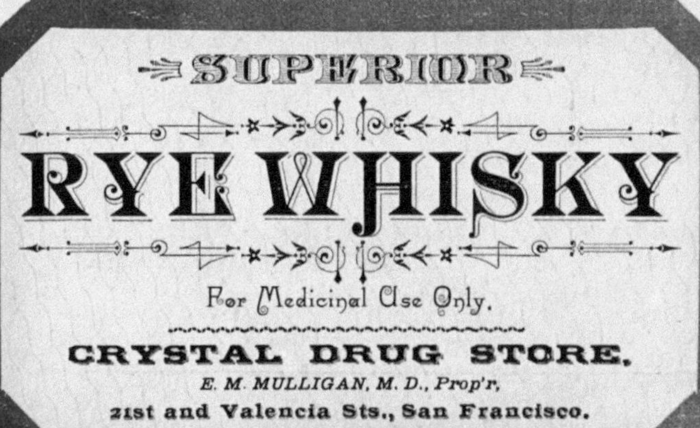

No. 4500—250, $1.25; 500, $1.75; 1000, $2.50. We do not print less than 250 to a name.

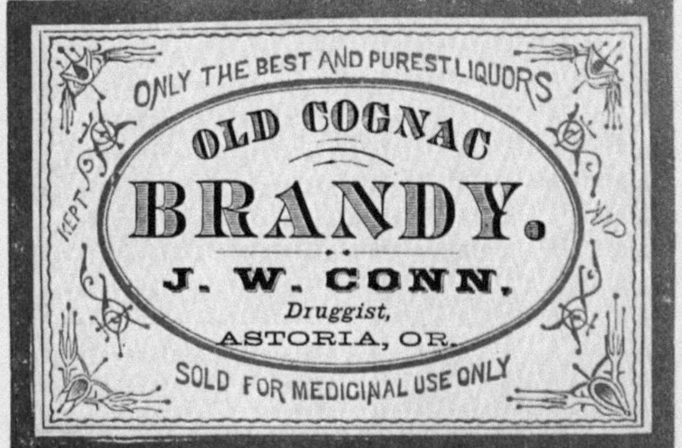

The names of any Wines or Liquors will be inserted, in any of the above Labels, without extra charge.

NOTE.—In this class of work we use four shades of coloring for Tint Grounds, viz: Slate, Pink, Blue and Green colors. Our aim is to assort them, but as this cannot always be done, we do not undertake to furnish any particular tint exclusively, or to give the same shade of tint a second time.

No. 4501—250, $1.25; 500, $1.75; 1000, $2.50.

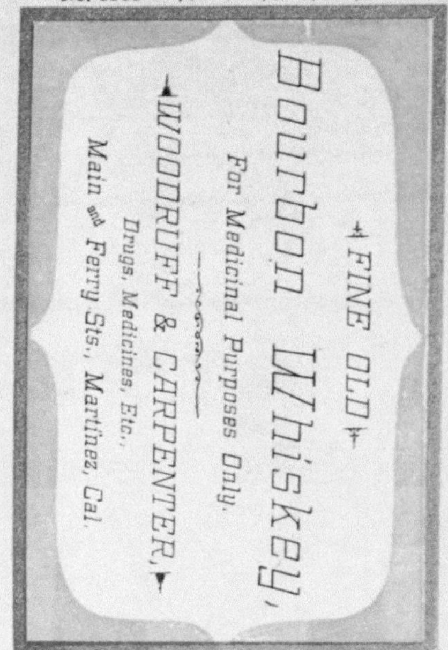

No. 4502—50, 30c; 100, 50c; 200, 85c; 500, $1.50; 1000, $2.50

In Pattern 4502 we keep the names of all Liquors in stock, at the prices quoted. See Note over Pattern 4498.

No. 4503—50, 25c; 100, 40c; 200, 60c; 500, $1.15; 1000, $2.00.

Miscellaneous Labels.

ORIGINAL TINTED GOLD SERIES.

THE marked favor with which this Series of Labels has been received has been highly gratifying to us, and we here present it showing an assortment of Tints for backgrounds, and a number of elegant new Labels that we have specially gotten up for these pages. The TINTED GOLD SERIES is particularly adapted for Toilet Specialties, and our large assortment of rules and borders enables us to furnish any size required, the border being printed in Gold and the reading matter in Black Ink. From the prices here quoted, the rates for corresponding sizes, with any reading matter, can be easily determined. These Labels are furnished Gummed and Cut, ready for use. In ordering, DO NOT cut up this Book, but write "TINTED GOLD SERIES" over Labels wanted in this style, give Number of Label, for size or reading, and we will understand the rest. We can not undertake to furnish either pattern of background or any color of tint EXCLUSIVELY, but aim to assort all.

＋IN THIS SERIES WE DO NOT PRINT LESS THAN 250 LABELS TO ANY ONE NAME OF ARTICLE.＋

No. 4372—250, $1.25; 500, $1.75; 1000, $2.50.　　　　No. 4373—250, $1.25; 500, $1.75; 1000, $2.50.　　　　No. 4374—250, $1.25; 500, $1.75; 1000, $2.50.

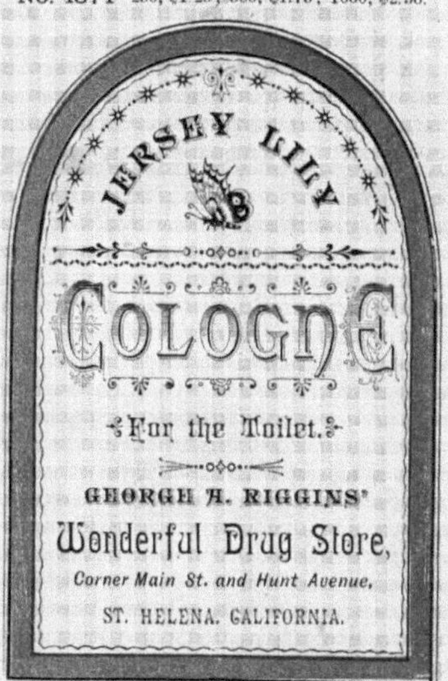

No. 4375—250, $1.50; 500, $2.00; 1000, $3.00.　　　　　　　No. 4376—250, $1.00; 500, $1.40; 1000, $2.00.

No. 4377—250, $1.75; 500, $2.35; 1000, $3.50.

Toilet Labels.

No. 4474.   Kept in Stock.   50, 35c; 100, 65c; 200, $1.10; 500, $2.00; 1000, $3.50.

No. 4475.   With address—100, $1.00; 200, $1.50; 500, $3.00; 1000, $4.50.   We do not furnish less than 100.

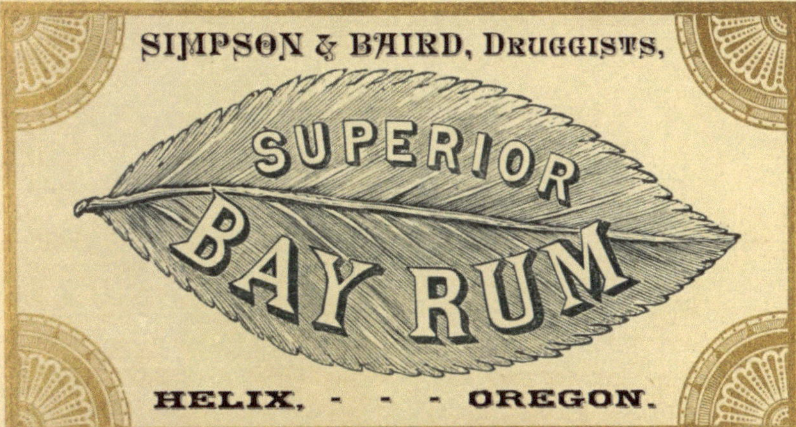

No. 4476.   Kept in Stock.   50, 40c; 100, 75c; 200, $1.25; 500, $2.50; 1000, $4.50.

No. 4477.   With address—100, 75c; 200, $1.00; 500, $1.50; 1000. $2.50.   We do not furnish less than 100.

No. 4478.   Kept in Stock at 15 cts per 100.

The above Label is furnished trimmed close to border.

No. 4479—250, $1.50; 500, $2.00; 1000, $3.00.

No. 4480—250, $1.75; 500, $2.35; 1000, $3.50.

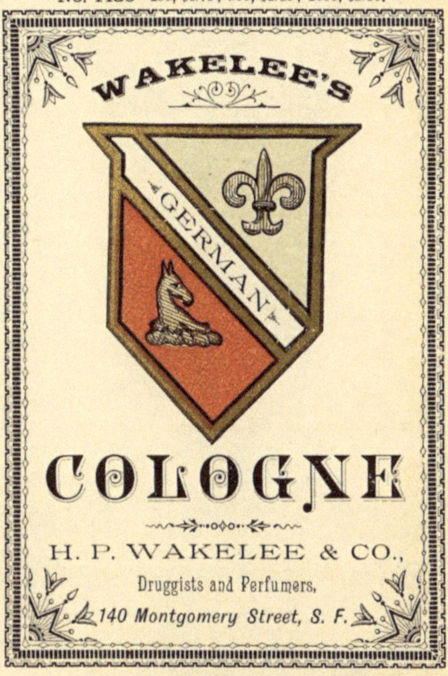

No. 4481—30c per 100.

In No. 4481 the name of any Toilet Article or Extract will be inserted at the same price.

No. 4482. With Address—100, $1.25; 200, $2.00; 500, $4.00; 1000, $6.50. We do not furnish a less quantity than 100.

No. 4484. 15c per 100.

No. 4483. With address—100, $1.00; 200, $1.50; 500, $3.00; 1000, $5.00. We do not furnish a less quantity than 100.

No. 4485. 15c per 100.

No. 4486.
250, 65c; 500, 90c; 1000, $1.30.

No. 4491. $1.00 per 100.

No. 4487. 35c per 100.

No. 4488. 15c per 100.

No. 4489. Kept in Stock at 50c per 100.

No. 4490. 35c per 100.

No. 4492. Kept in Stock at 50c per 100.

Sherry Wine, Jamaica Rum and Bourbon Whisky Labels, in the above pattern, kept in Stock at same rates.

All the above Toilet Labels are printed on fine white writing paper, and are cut close up to borders by machinery without extra charge. These Labels are only furnished ungummed.

DO NOT cut or mutilate this Specimen Book, but order by Number of the Pattern, writing out the names of articles desired.

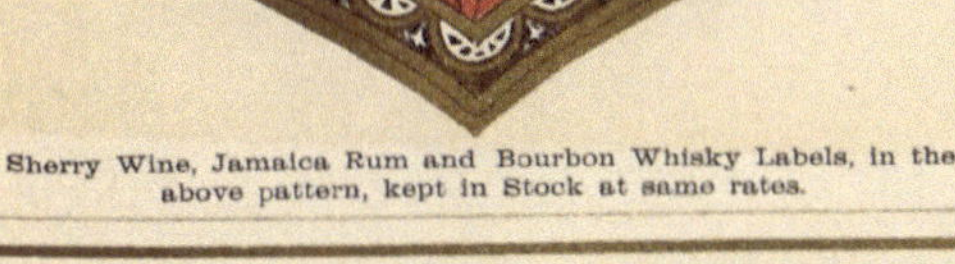

Hair Oil and Bay Rum Labels, in the above pattern, kept in Stock at same rates.

Liquor Labels.

No. 4493—250, $1.25; 500, $1.75; 1000, $2.50.

No. 4494—250, $1.50; 500, $2.00; 1000, $3.00.

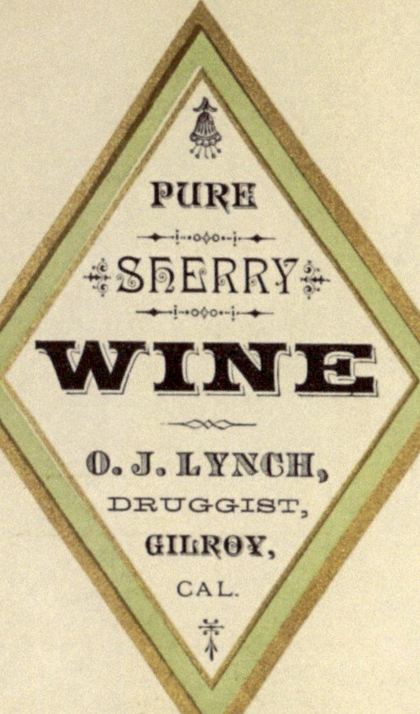

The names of any Wines or Liquors will be inserted, in any of the Labels shown on this page, without extra charge.

No. 4495—250, $1.25; 500, $1.75; 1000, $2.50.

J. H. HARDING, DRUGGIST,

COGNAC BRANDY

COMPTON, - - CALIFORNIA.

No. 4497—250, $1.50; 500, $2.00; 1000, $3.00.

No. 4496.   Kept in Stock.   50, 30c; 100, 50c; 200, 85c; 500, $1.50; 1000, $2.50.

SUPERIOR

BOURBON WHISKY

FOR MEDICINAL USE.

NOTE.—In this class of work we use four shades of coloring for Tint Grounds, viz: Green, Blue, Pink and Slate colors. Our aim is to assort them, but as this cannot always be done, we do not undertake to furnish any particular tint exclusively, or to give the same shade of tint a second time.

McNeil Bros., San Jose, Cal.

Prescription Blanks.

No. 4504. 500, $2.50; 1000, $4.00; 2000, $6.75; 3000, $9.25; 5000, $13.50.

No. 4505. 500, $2.75; 1000, $4.50; 2000, $7.50; 3000, $10.25; 5000, $15.00.

T. I. McKENNY,

Druggist and Apothecary,

McKenny's Block, Olympia, W. T.

No. .... Date,

For ....

R

M. D.

PHYSICIANS' PRESCRIPTIONS CAREFULLY COMPOUNDED.

NOTE.—In this class of work we use four shades of coloring for Tint Grounds, viz: Blue, Green, Pink and Slate colors. Our aim is to assort them, but as this cannot always be done, we do not undertake to furnish any particular tint exclusively, or to give the same shade of tint a second time.

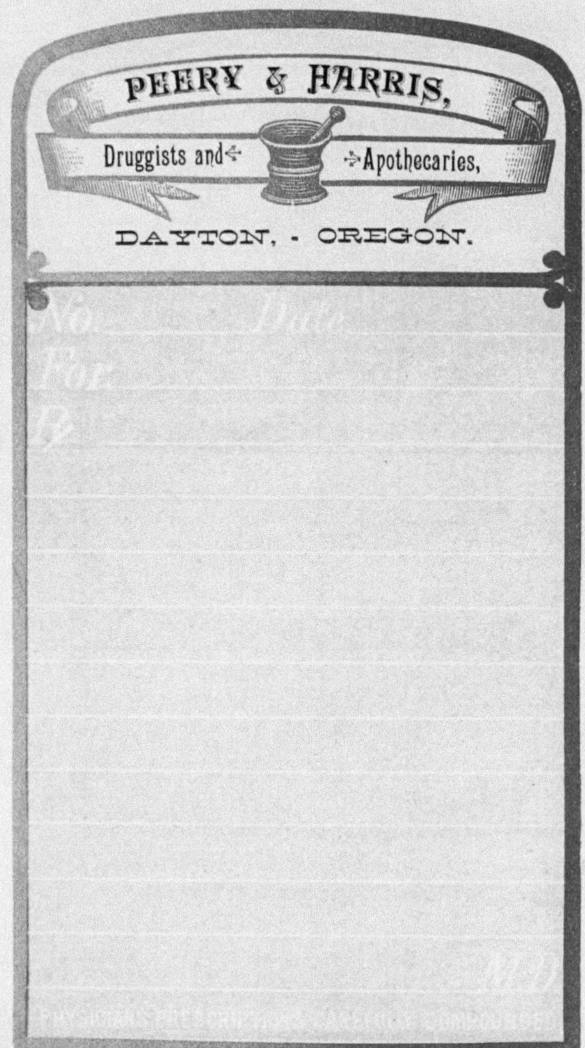

No. 4506. 500, $2.25; 1000, $3.50; 2000, $6.00; 3000, $8.25; 5000, $12.00.

PRICES FOR BINDING
Prescription Blanks.

The prices here given are for loose Prescription Blanks. We bind them in various styles and at prices as follows:

IN TABLETS, (or Pads), of 100 each, neatly finished with ornamental paper and colored edges— 1000 or less, at 5 cts per Tablet; 2000, at 4½ cts per Tablet; 3000 and over, at 4 cts per Tablet. If bound 50 Blanks each, same price per Tablet.

IN BOOKS, perforated on end for tearing off, with good substantial covers and colored edges— any number of Books under 30, 8 cts each. Over 30 Books, 7 cts each. For "Acme" Prescription Case, with backs cut ready for pocket, 7 cts each.

We also bind in Book form with tough, flexible covers, at 10 cts each. This is a very convenient form for pocket use.

IMITATION MOROCCO Covers, 12 cts per Book extra. This is a handsome, strong binding, for office or desk.

FULL MOROCCO Covers, with loops for pencils, 50 cts each. The name of any physician can be stamped in gold upon the side of this Cover, at an extra cost of 15 cts for each name.

A Physician's name can be inserted on any Prescription Blank without extra charge; but if more than one name is ordered, an additional charge of 20 Cents will be made for each name.

When specially ordered, Stubs are furnished to all Prescription Blanks, at the rate of 50 cts extra for the first 1000, and 25c for each additional 1000.

McNeil Bros., San Jose, Cal.

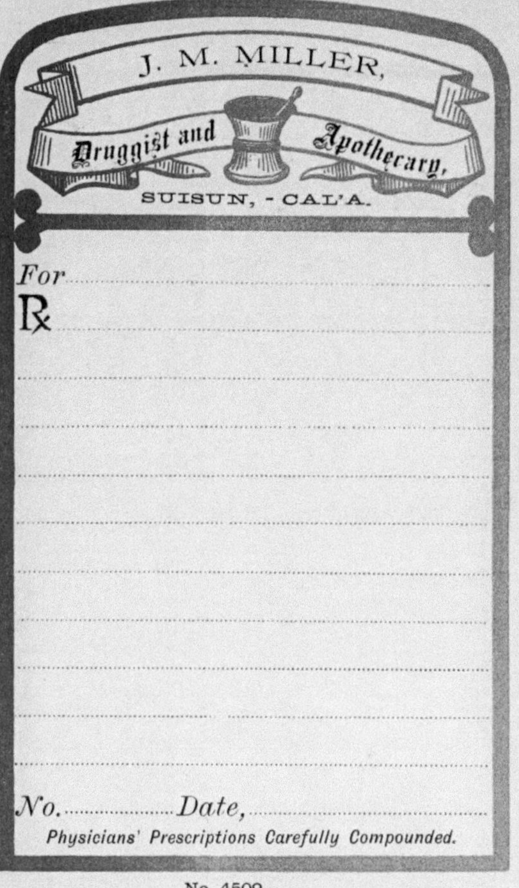

NOTE.—In this class of work we use four shades of coloring for Tint Grounds, viz: Blue, Green, Pink and Slate colors. Our aim is to assort them, but as this cannot always be done, we do not undertake to furnish any particular tint exclusively, or to give the same shade of tint a second time.

Prices for Binding

PRESCRIPTION BLANKS.

The prices here given are for loose Prescription Blanks. We bind them in various styles, and at prices as follows:

IN TABLETS, (or Pads), of 100 each, neatly finished with ornamental paper and colored edges—1000 or less, at 5 cts per Tablet; 2000, at 4½ cts per Tablet; 3000 and over, at 4 cts per Tablet. If bound 50 Blanks each, same price per Tablet.

IN BOOKS, perforated on end for tearing off, with good substantial covers and colored edges—any number of Books under 30, at 8 cts each. Over 30 Books, 7 cts each. For "Acme" Prescription Case, with backs cut ready for pocket, 7 cts each.

We also bind in Book form, with tough, flexible covers, at 10 cts each. This is a very convenient form for pocket use.

IMITATION MOROCCO Covers, 12 cts per Book extra. A handsome, strong binding, for office or desk.

FULL MOROCCO Covers, with loops for pencils, 50 cts each. The name of Physician can be stamped in gold upon the side of this Cover, at an extra cost of 15 cts for each name.

A Physician's name can be inserted on any Prescription Blank without extra charge; but if more than one name is ordered, an additional charge of 20 Cents will be made for each name.

When specially ordered, Stubs are furnished to all Prescription Blanks, at the rate of 50 cts extra for the first 1000, and 25 cts for each additional 1000.